WORLD OF
MAMMALS

ZEBRAS

By Sophie Lockwood

Content Adviser: Barbara E. Brown, Scientific Associate, Mammal Division, Field Museum of Chicago

THE CHILD'S WORLD®, MANKATO, MINNESOTA

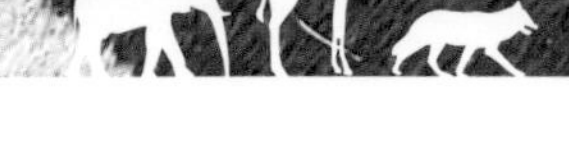

Zebras

Published in the United States of America by The Child's World®
1980 Lookout Drive • Mankato, MN 56003-1705
800-599-READ • www.childsworld.com

Acknowledgements:

The Child's World®: Mary Berendes, Publishing Director

The Creative Spark: Mary Francis, Project Director; Wendy Mead, Editor; Deborah Goodsite, Photo Researcher

The Design Lab: Kathleen Petelinsek, Designer and Production Artist

Photos:

Cover and half title: James Warwick/Getty Images; frontispiece and page 4: Jamie Wilson/ iStockphoto.com.

Interior: AP Photo: 30 (Karel Prinsloo); Corbis: 5 bottom left and 29 (Bettmann); Getty: 32 (Stringer/AFP), 35 (Heinrich van den Berg/Gallo Images); iStockphoto.com: 5 top left and 9 (Liz Leyden), 5 top right and11 (Nico Smit), 5 center left and 15 (Mark Weiss); Minden Pictures: 12 (Mitsuaki Iwago), 21 (Konrad Wothe); Peter Arnold, Inc.: 19 (Jean-Michel Labat/PHONE), 23 (Martin Harvey); Photolibrary Group: 16, 5 bottom right and 24, 26, 36 -37.

Library of Congress Cataloging-in-Publication Data

Lockwood, Sophie.
Zebras / by Sophie Lockwood.
p. cm. — (The world of mammals)
Includes index.
ISBN 978-1-59296-931-9 (library bound : alk. paper)
1. Zebras—Juvenile literature. I. Title. II. Series.
QL737.U62L63 2008
599.665'7—dc22 2007021689

TABLE OF CONTENTS

chapter one | **ON THE SERENGETI PLAIN** | 6

chapter two | **HERDS, HAREMS, AND HERMITS** | 10

chapter three | **A LIFE IN STRIPES** | 14

chapter four | **TYPES OF ZEBRAS** | 18

chapter five | **THE PAST, PRESENT, AND FUTURE** | 28

Glossary, 38

For More Information, 39

The Animal Kingdom—Where Do Zebras Fit In?, 39

Index, 40

Chapter One

On the Serengeti Plain

The dry season is finally coming to an end on the Serengeti Plain. The heat is unbearable. The grass has dried up, and water holes have become dry hollows of hard, sunbaked soil.

To the west, thick, gray clouds gather. Heat lightning slices through the sky. Thunder rumbles over the land. Fire! Lightning has struck the earth, and fire bursts yellow and red and orange. The fire races toward the Mara River and stops at the river's edge.

The fire leaves behind a fine, **nutrient**-rich layer of ash. A soft drizzle begins. The thirsty soil soaks up the gentle rain like a sponge. The drizzle changes quickly to a full-blown storm. Streams fill and water pours into water holes. Runoff water feeds the Mara.

Tomorrow, new grass will grow on the Serengeti. Tomorrow, a massive herd of zebras, wildebeests, and antelopes—more than two million animals—will move toward that sprouting grass. The herds will start their yearly 483-kilometer (300-mile) **migration.**

Did You Know?
Just like horses, male zebras are called stallions, females are called mares, and their young are called foals.

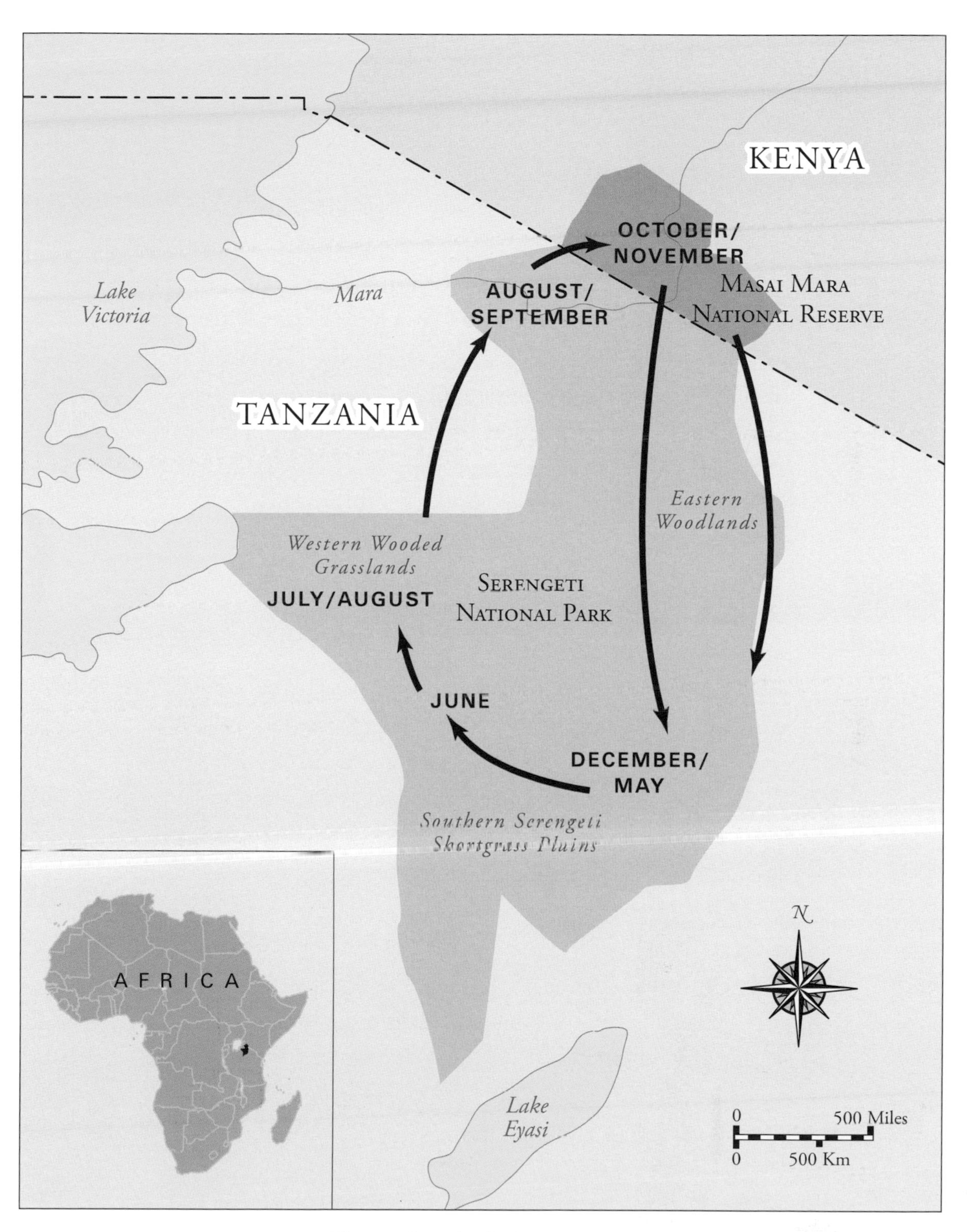

This map shows the zebras' migratory route.

Did You Know?
Zebras pack a wallop with their hooves. A strong kick in the ribs can cause serious injuries to **predators.** Even lions keep clear of a zebra's hooves.

The herd must cross the Mara, a river teeming with Nile crocodiles. A few wildebeests timidly enter the river, and then the herd crashes through the water. Zebras swim across. Beneath the rushing brown water, a crocodile lurks. The 5-meter (16-foot) monster snatches a zebra's leg in its jaws. Crushing the leg, the crocodile pulls the zebra underwater to its death. Yet for every zebra taken, hundreds more cross the Mara successfully.

By the time the herd arrives on the Serengeti, the grass has reached at least 60 centimeters (2 feet) high. Zebras stick close to wildebeests and antelopes. There is safety in large numbers. An adult zebra feeding alone might fall prey to lions, hyenas, or packs of African wild dogs. In the herd, some animal is always watching, always alert, and always ready to issue a warning. A bark or yelp announces that predators are near.

Zebras, wildebeests, and antelopes eat grass, but they do not compete for food. Zebras have strong, sharp **incisors** that snip the top levels of grass. Wildebeests eat the middle levels, and antelopes browse on low-lying herbs and new grass sprouts. Therefore, all three species can feed together in the same grassland.

Serengeti zebras belong to the common or plains zebra species (*Equus burchelli*). Although they travel in the midst

of a sprawling herd, zebras actually live in small family units called harems. A single stallion protects a handful of mares and foals from predators and other stallions. During the migration, the oldest mare leads the way, followed by other mares and the foals. The stallion brings up the rear so that he can act if danger threatens. To make sure that no family members get lost during the migration, the family moves at the pace of its slowest member.

Once on the Serengeti Plain, zebras will graze until the dry season dries up the water holes and scorches the grass. The herd moves as food grows scarce. The migration is part of the constant cycle of life revolving on the African **savanna.**

Zebras cross the Mara River as part of their migration.

Would You Believe?
Zebras take dirt baths to get rid of lice, insects, and dry skin. They find a patch of rough, dry ground and roll on their backs. Other animals can also help them stay clean. A yellow-billed oxpecker will sit on a zebra and will eat ticks, flies, and fleas. This helps to get rid of **parasites.**

Chapter Two

Herds, Harems, and Hermits

Africa has three species of zebras, which are plains zebras, mountain zebras (*Equus zebra*), and Grevy's zebras (*Equus grevyi*). Each species has its own social structure and lifestyle. Some harems join large herds, and some remain by themselves. In some situations, the females move about in groups, but the stallions live alone, like hermits.

Plains and mountain zebras have stable family units. When a stallion reaches adulthood, he looks for young, unattached mares. As a mare becomes mature, she goes into **estrus.** When this happens for the first time, the mare stands in a peculiar way. A stallion that notices this stance will try to separate her from her family and mate with her.

The stallion and mare will form the core of a new family group. Among plains zebras, a stallion and his mares remain together for life. This bond is unusual for herd

animals. The first mare in the harem is the **dominant,** or head, female. The newest female has the lowest social status.

This Cape mountain zebra is taking a chance feeding alone. It is more open to attack from lions or hyenas.

Did You Know?
A group of zebras on a plain often form a circle facing outward. In that way, the zebras can see an approaching predator.

Stallions may control a territory for fifteen or more years. When the stallion dies, a lucky young stallion may take his place as harem leader. The mares remain together.

Mountain zebras gather in harems but do not usually form large herds. Grass is scarce where mountain zebras live, so

Did You Know?
A mother zebra keeps her newborn foal away from the rest of the harem for two or three days so the youngster can learn her stripe pattern and smell.

Two male Grant's zebras fight on the Serengeti Plain.

it would not be possible to feed a large herd. Harems are smaller, usually only a stallion, two or three mares, and their **offspring.** Stallions that do not have harems or access to mates live in bachelor groups.

Would You Believe?
When stallions fight for territory, they compete aggressively. They kick and bite and can cause serious damage to their rivals.

Grevy's zebras do not form tight-knit family units. The social unit is not a harem, but a nursing mare and one or two foals. The older foal is a **juvenile** that is not yet mature enough to leave its mother.

Grevy's stallions stick to one piece of land, protecting their grazing area and water hole rights. They mate with mares that pass through their territory. If no females are around, the stallion may join other bachelors.

Among zebra species, colts and fillies (young males and females) leave the family group when they reach adulthood. Mares are not ready to produce young until they are two to three years old. They will be "kidnapped" by a stallion to join a new harem. Colts reach maturity at four to five years old. Males leave their family unit and join bachelor groups of five to fifteen stallions. They are waiting for their opportunities to start harems of their own.

Chapter Three

A Life in Stripes

An eight-year-old stallion challenges a much older stallion for the senior zebra's harem. The challenge is physical, demanding, and dangerous. The two stallions go at each other with teeth bared. They bite each other's necks and legs. They deliver kicks that could easily crack ribs. The battles between two stallions can produce fatal injuries. This time, the younger stallion wins, and the older one must leave the harem. The young stallion snorts and stamps. He has won mating rights to two mares.

The stallion separates a mare from her family unit. She will never return. From that time on, the mare has a new family and new responsibilities. When she becomes pregnant, she will carry her foal for a full year.

A newborn gets to its feet within six to fourteen minutes of being born. Within an hour, the newborn can run with its family group. This is important because the calf must be able to run with the herd to escape from predators. Within a week, the foal

Would You Believe?
Zebras can gallop at 55 kilometers per hour (35 miles per hour) and can run at 80 kilometers per hour (50 miles per hour) for short distances.

begins nibbling grasses. The baby weighs between 25 and 40 kilograms (55 to 88 pounds). Newborn zebras have brown stripes that darken to black with age. They stay close to their mothers and drink mother's milk for ten to twelve months.

Protecting the foals is a full-time job. In harems with stallions, the males help keep foals safe. In smaller groups of just mares and their offspring, the mother plays the role of prime protector. Near the water hole, a lion hides in the reeds. A mare keeps a careful watch as her colt drinks. She snorts in alarm as the lion sneaks closer. Her ears lowered, she gets ready to kick if an attack occurs. Luckily, she and the colt leave the water hole unharmed.

Because they need to drink regularly, zebras rarely roam far from a water hole.

Zebras spend about two-thirds of every day munching and chewing grasses. They feed early in the morning and at dusk. During summer months, the heat becomes intense. Most zebras remain inactive when the afternoon sun burns its hottest.

Did You Know?
The zebra is the only grazing animal that has both upper and lower incisors. These sharp teeth allow the zebra to snip grass rather than pull the grass out by the roots.

A plains zebra foal searches for food with its mother at sunrise.

Would You Believe?
Zebras are attracted to black-and-white stripes. If a zoo has a black-and-white striped wall, zebras stand near it.

When not eating, zebras catch up on their sleep. During the day, zebras may sleep standing up. As night falls, many zebras lie down to nap. While they do so, other zebras stand guard. A sleeping zebra is defenseless. When a guard whinnies a warning, a zebra goes from asleep to full gallop in seconds.

Zebras have a strong fight-or-flight response. When there is a threat, they run. The **instinct** to flee is strong, and even the youngest zebra kicks into high speed when danger lurks. That danger comes from such animals as lions, leopards, cheetahs, hyenas, and African wild dogs, which prey on zebras. Crocodiles nab zebras when the zebras cross rivers or drink at a river's edge. Although rare, hippopotamuses have also been known to kill zebras during river crossings.

Stripes play an important part in a zebra's survival. They are more than decoration. A running herd of zebras looks like a blur to predators, as the stripes seem to race across the land. Zebra stripes seem clear to humans because we see in color. Most predators, however, see only in black-and-white. To them, zebras blend in with high grass. When zebras group together, predators cannot tell where one zebra begins and another ends. Stripes are lifesavers.

Chapter Four

Types of Zebras

Each zebra has its own personal stripe pattern, and the general stripe pattern is different from species to species. Different species also differ in their size, their vocal sounds, and the places where they live. Horses and zebras both belong to the **genus** *Equus*. While they are cousins, zebras and horses are not alike. Horses, for the most part, are easily trained and can be ridden by humans. Zebras resist training, and only rarely can a zebra be tamed sufficiently so that humans can ride it.

The plains zebra family includes a host of subspecies, including Chapman's, Crawshay's, Damara, Grant's, and Upper Zambezi zebras. Sturdy and round-bodied, male plains zebras weigh about 300 kilograms (660 pounds) and stand 127 to 140 centimeters (50 to 55 inches) tall. The females are slightly smaller. They weigh 220 kilograms (485 pounds) and stand a bit shorter.

Plain zebras have white or buff bodies with bold black stripes. One of the

Would You Believe?
Some scientists think that zebra stripes confuse the tsetse fly, a bothersome pest that usually avoids zebras.

boldest stripe patterns is found on Crawshay's zebras. They have vertical stripes on their necks and bodies. Stripes on the rump and legs are horizontal. Some plains zebras also have faint gray markings, or shadow stripes, between their wide black stripes.

Plains zebras can be found on open savanna or semi-arid land from Sudan to South Africa and as far west as Angola. They thrive in fairly dry conditions, but they do need regular access to water.

A Grant's zebra calls out in the Masai Mara region of Kenya.

Did You Know?
Male Grevy's zebras let outsiders know the boundaries of their territories by marking the borders with large piles of dung, called middens.

GREVY'S ZEBRAS

The Grevy's zebra is the largest zebra species as well as the largest wild horse species. Some people think that it is the most beautiful type of zebra. Adults reach shoulder heights of 150 centimeters (4.9 feet) and weigh 400 kilograms (880 pounds) or more. It is easy to tell a Grevy's zebra from other zebra species—they have narrow black stripes. The species has large rounded ears and a short mane that stands straight up. Their heads and necks are long, while their legs are surprisingly thin.

Grevy's zebras live in semiarid, thorny bushland. They can be found in Kenya, Somalia, and Ethiopia. Although the Grevy's zebra's range overlaps that of the plains zebra, the two species are rarely seen together. Living in or near the desert means that Grevy's zebras must travel to visit water holes. They generally drink at dawn and dusk, when their stripes make them hard to see in the dim light.

MOUNTAIN ZEBRAS

The easiest way to tell if a zebra is a mountain zebra is to look for a square flap of skin, called a dewlap, on the throat. As their name implies, mountain zebras live in rugged mountains, along ravines, and in territory where few

other grazers can survive. The two subspecies of mountain zebras are Cape mountain zebras (*Equus zebra zebra*) and Hartmann's zebras (*Equus zebra hartmannae*).

Two Hartmann's zebras, a mother and foal, wander in a national park in Namibia.

Did You Know?
Cape mountain zebras were endangered when South Africa established the Mountain Zebra National Park. Breeding rates at the park are high, with thirty-two new foals born yearly to every one hundred mares.

Cape mountain zebras stand about 12 centimeters (4.7 inches) shorter than Hartmann's zebras. They are the shortest zebras but also the roundest ones, with stocky, squat bodies, and long ears. Cape mountain zebras have adjusted so well to living on sheer cliffs and rugged mountains that they travel safely in areas where only wild goats and sheep live. Cape mountain zebras live in South Africa, where food and water are always available.

Hartmann's zebras, on the other hand, live in drier mountain areas and travel around a lot in search of food. They have wide black stripes on white or buff bodies. The stripes go all the way down the legs but do not meet on the belly. Hartmann's zebras stand up to 132 centimeters (52 inches) high at the shoulder. They are playful animals, racing each other and engaging in play fights. Both Cape mountain and Hartmann's zebras are good climbers and can live for twenty years in the wild.

QUAGGAS

One problem scientists studying zebras faced was with naming the animals they had discovered. Two scientists found animals they believed had never been recorded. They each named their animals. The scientists were actually

describing the same species, so the zebra wound up with two names. The quagga and the true Burchell's quagga were once considered distinct animals. Scientists now believe that both were what is today called the quagga.

Quaggas were large, brown and buff striped zebras. They lived in South Africa below the Orange River. The quagga disappeared from the wild by 1878, most likely hunted to **extinction.** The last living quagga died in a zoo in 1883. Today, scientists have begun an experimental breeding program using Chapman's zebras to try to recreate quaggas from their DNA.

This is a quagga foal on display in a South African museum.

The Przewalski's horse is a wild horse much like the zebra.

A ZEBRA'S RELATIVES: WILD HORSES

Zebras are equids—horses. Although millions of farm-bred horses can be found throughout the world, wild horses are rare. They include zebras, Przewalski's horses, kiangs, and African and Asiatic wild asses.

The Przewalski's (sheh-VAHL-skeez) horse is officially listed as extinct in the wild. This small horse once roamed from the Ural Mountains of Russia to Mongolia. A few may still live in remote areas in the Altai Mountains, along the border between Mongolia and Siberia. These horses have stocky bodies, low-set shoulders, and brownish tan coats. They stand 120 centimeters (3.9 feet) from hoof to shoulder. Small zoo populations exist and are part of captive breeding programs in England, Russia, China, and Mongolia. They are even being reintroduced into the wild in Mongolia now.

The kiang (kee-YAHNG) is a wild ass that lives on the Tibetan plateau in Asia. Kiangs have reddish-brown backs and rumps, with white or buff bellies, chests, and legs. They measure 140 centimeters (4.6 feet) at the shoulder. They live in tight-knit herds of five to four hundred individuals based on the relationships between the females. Because kiangs live

Did You Know?
Zebras, asses, and horses used to have three toes. Long ago, these toes fused together or got smaller. Today these animals walk on one toe—we call it a hoof.

in such remote areas, little is known about how many of them actually exist.

Wild asses live in Africa and Asia. The African variety is buff-gray in the summer months and iron-gray during the winter. In appearance, they are much like large donkeys. African asses live in hilly country, stony deserts, bushland, and grassland in small groups of five or fewer animals. Males usually live alone. Stable

Did You Know?
The African wild ass is among the world's rarest animals, with an estimated 2002 population of fewer than 570 animals.

No one is certain how many kiangs there are because they live in a wilderness area.

family units are most commonly made of a mare and one or two young. Wild asses can be found in Ethiopia, Eritrea, and Somalia, but their populations are very small. There is also some question about whether these are true wild asses. They may be domestic asses that have returned to the wild.

There are marked differences between wild asses and horses. Although both species collect in herds, wild horses tend to be active during the day while asses are active at night. This may be because wild asses tend to live in hotter climates, such as African and Asian deserts. Shorter and lighter weight than horses, wild asses prefer to run away from predators than to fight them. They do bite and kick but are not as successful in defending themselves as wild horses are.

Asiatic asses include several subspecies, including Mongolian, Persian, and Indian wild asses. The Mongolian ass is also called a kulan. Persian asses are called onagers and there are only about four hundred of them left in the wild. Indian asses are known as khurs. Khurs living near the Arabian Sea are also endangered in the wild. The last known surviving wild herd roams the salt plains along the India-Pakistan border. It is believed that there are about two thousand khurs left. Asiatic asses generally have dark brown or gray backs, rumps, and flanks, and white muzzles, chests, and underbellies. They closely resemble burros or donkeys.

Chapter Five

The Past, Present, and Future

No one knows how long zebras have lived on Africa's dry hills and plains. Fossil remains of Grevy's zebras date back six thousand years. Two thousand years ago, zebras appeared in Roman circuses and in European zoos. Zebras have fascinated people for centuries.

Today, Grevy's zebras and mountain zebras are endangered. The major obstacle to their survival is man. Plains zebras are still plentiful and will stay so as long as access to open savanna remains.

The primary problem is loss of habitat. Zebras are **nomads.** They roam over fairly large areas for their food and water. Unfortunately, this habit conflicts with human developments. For humans, if the choice is maintaining grazing and water areas for their livestock or for zebras, the zebras lose.

Would You Believe?
Grevy's zebras got their name from Jules Grévy, president of the French Republic. Grévy received a live zebra in 1882 as a gift from Menelik II of Abyssinia. After the animal died, it was stuffed. Photos of it were sent to London, labeled "Grevy's zebra." The species has been known as Grevy's zebra since then.

A group of hunters stand with the zebras they killed.

THREATS TO SURVIVAL

The decline of the Grevy's zebra population began in the 1960s. The zebras were hunted for meat and skins, or access to water holes during droughts were denied.

These zebras graze in the Nairobi National Park, with the growing city of Nairobi closing in around them.

Poorly run **ecotourism** is another problem Grevy's zebras face. Off-road vehicles allow tourists access to herds but disturb the animals and affect breeding.

Grevy's zebras are now extinct in Somalia, and herds are greatly reduced in Ethiopia and Kenya. The total wild population may have fallen to fewer than 2,500 Grevy's zebras.

The story in the 1930s for mountain zebras was much as the same as for Grevy's zebras today. Zebra populations suffered losses because of trophy hunting and poaching. Again, zebras were denied access to water, grasslands, and crop fields. Advancing human settlements destroyed natural zebra territory with villages and farms, which caused more problems. Zebras happily munch on leafy shrubs and cannot tell wild varieties from tidy rows of farm crops.

Because of these problems, mountain zebra populations declined by nearly 50 percent in ten years. Something had to be done to save these beautiful animals.

CONSERVATION

Fortunately for zebras, their stunning appearance makes them popular **conservation** species. Zebras are flagship species and umbrella species. A flagship species is a species that attracts support from people

Did You Know?
Zebras say "hello" to each other with a smile. They bare their teeth in a kind of grin that is used as a greeting.

because the animal in question is popular. Zebras are stars in the conservation world. An umbrella species is one that protects many other creatures simply because the species' normal habitat covers a large area. To protect an umbrella species, large tracts of land must be protected. All animals

Staff from Lewa Wildlife Conservancy load a group of zebras onto a truck to move them to a new location.

Did You Know?
You can adopt a zebra! The Smithsonian National Zoo runs a program that allows people to adopt Grevy's zebras. Contact the zoo to find out how you can help save this animal.

and plants living on that preserve also become protected.

Several organizations are working together to save the Grevy's zebra. In 1977, the Kenyan government banned zebra hunting. Although poaching still occurs, the general slaughter of zebras has slowed dramatically. In addition, CITES, the Convention on International Trade in Endangered Species, banned the sale of zebra skins and body parts worldwide. Reducing the market for zebra skins also reduces the profit for poachers.

Conservation groups, such as the African Wildlife Foundation and the Lewa Wildlife Conservancy, have begun to study Grevy's zebras. They educate local people about preserving zebras rather than killing them. Part of this effort is aimed at getting the status of zebras changed from game to legally protected species. The African Wildlife Foundation's Grevy's zebra project works with local communities to track the movement of zebras in the Samburu Heartland of Kenya. By understanding where the zebras go and when, the group hopes to develop a plan to ensure the continued safety of the wild Samburu herd.

The Lewa Wildlife Conservancy is a 25,900-hectare (100-square-mile), privately owned preserve in Kenya dedicated to saving African wildlife. About five hundred

Grevy's zebras roam the conservancy's land, along with many other animals.

The plight of the mountain zebras became serious in the 1930s. In 1937, the South African government established the Mountain Zebra National Park on the northern slopes of the Blankberg mountain range. The park was created particularly to save the mountain zebra, although the zebras have plenty of contented neighbors, including kudus, caracals, jackals, springboks, and bonteboks.

By 1964, the population of mountain zebra had reached a low of twenty-five animals. Today, the herd has more than two hundred members. In addition, many more mountain zebras have been released into other national parks to form starter herds. Today, about six hundred mountain zebras live throughout their original natural range.

Life in Mountain Zebra National Park is not without its perils. Aardwolves chow down on thousands of termites daily. Caracals slink through the scrub, looking for rodents, birds, and small deer. Tiny Cape foxes seek out lizards and rabbits. But zebra predators, such as lions, hyenas, and leopards, do not live in the park, so park zebras are safe.

Tourists love zebras. Many people pay to vacation in places where they can see zebras in the wild. The fact that people will pay to observe zebras helps secure the animals'

future. That money can be used to safeguard the land and its animals, as well as to provide support for the people living in the region.

The government of South Africa established a special park to help mountain zebras, such as the Cape mountain zebras shown here, survive.

Without help from humans, zebras may become extinct.

Many zebras live in zoos, and maintaining a healthy captive population of Grevy's and mountain zebras is important. The Association of Zoos and Aquariums has species survival plans in place for Hartmann's zebras and Grevy's zebras. The plan calls for promoting careful captive breeding in zoos. Male zebras are traded among different zoos to develop zebra population with a wide **genetic** base.

Humans are both the problem and the solution for zebra survival. We can only hope that our conservation efforts have come in time to save these magnificent animals. With the help of preserved habitats and protective laws, zebras hopefully will roam the African savannas for many years to come.

Glossary

conservation (kon-sur-VAY-shun) the preservation or management of natural resources

dominant (DOM-ih-nunt) in control or command of others

ecotourism (ee-koh-TOOR-izm) a form of tourism that strives to minimize damage to areas visited for their natural interest, such as a coral reef or a rainforest

estrus (ESS-truss) a period during which female mammals are ready to mate

extinction (eks-TINK-shun) the state of a plant or animal no longer existing

genetic (jeh-NEH-tik) the study of the chemical substances that make up animal or plant characteristics

genus (JEE-nuss) a category used for classifying animals and plants into like groups

incisors (in-SY-zurz) flat, sharp-edged teeth in the front of the mouth

instinct (IN-stihnkt) one's natural sense of what is happening with one's body or actions one takes

juvenile (JOO-vuh-nyl) young or youthful

migration (my-GRAY-shun) the act of moving from one location to another, usually to live

nomads (NOH-madz) people or animals that travel regularly and have no fixed home, nest, or den

nutrient (NOO-tree-unt) a substance that provides nourishment

offspring (OFF-spring) the young of a species

parasites (PAYR-uh-sites) plants or animals that live on or in another, usually larger, host plant or animal, such as a tick or flea living on a zebra

predators (PREH-duh-turz) animals that hunt and kill other animals for food

savanna (suh-VAN-nuh) a grassy plain

For More Information

Watch It

Families in the Wild, VHS (Thousand Oaks, CA: Goldhil Home Media, 2001)

Nature: Serengeti Stories, VHS (New York: Thirteen/WNET: 2000)

Zebras: Patterns in the Grass, VHS (Washington, DC: National Geographic, 1997)

Read It

Macaulay, Kelley, and Bobbie Kalman. *Endangered Zebras*. New York: Crabtree Children's Books, 2007.

Markert, Jenny. *Zebras*. Mankato, MN: The Child's World, 2007.

Markle, Sandra. *Animal Prey: Zebras*. Minneapolis, MN: Lerner Publications, 2007.

Stewart, Melissa. *Zebras*. Danbury, CT: Children's Press, 2002.

Thompson, Gare. *Science Chapters: Serengeti Journey: On Safari in Africa*. Washington, DC: National Geographic Books for Children, 2006.

Look It Up

Visit our Web page for lots of links about zebras:
http://www.childsworld.com/links

Note to Parents, Teachers, and Librarians: We routinely verify our Web links to make sure they are safe, active sites—so encourage your readers to check them out!

The Animal Kingdom
Where Do Zebras Fit In?

Kingdom: Animalia
Phylum: Chordata (animals with backbones)
Class: Mammalia
Order: Perissodactyla
Family: Equidae
Genus: *Equus*

Species: *Equus zebra*
Equus burchelli
Equus quagga (extinct)
Equus grevyi

Index

adulthood, 10, 13
African Wildlife Foundation, 33
Association of Zoos and Aquariums, 37

bachelor groups, 13
breeding programs, 23

Cape mountain zebras, *11*, 21, *35*
captive breeding, 37
Chapman's zebras, 18
CITES (Convention on International Trade in Endangered Species), 33
color, 17, 26
colts, 13
common zebras. *See* plains zebras.
communication, 8, 17, 18, *19*, 31
conservation, 31–35, *32*, 37
Crawshay's zebras, 18, 19

Damara zebras, 18
dewlaps, 20
dirt baths, 9
dominant females, 11

ecotourism, 31
endangered species, 22
equids, 25
Equus genus, 18
estrus, 10
extinction, 23, 25, 31, *36*

farming, 28, 31
females. *See* fillies; mares.
fighting, 13, 14
fillies, 13
flagship species, 31–32
foals, 9, 12, 13, 14–15, *21*, 27
food. *See* grazing.
fossils, 28

Grant's zebras, *12*, 18, *19*
grazing, 8, *8*, 9, *9*, *11*, 12–13, 16, *16*
Grévy, Jules, 28
Grevy's zebras, 10, 13, 20, 28, 30–31, 33, 34, 37
grooming, 9

habitats, 20–21, 22, 25, 26, 27, 28, 37
harems, 9, 10–11, 12, 13, 14
Hartmann's zebras, 21, *21*, 22
height, 18, 20, 22, 25
humans, 18, 28, *29*, *32*

khurs, 27
kiangs, 25–26, *26*
kicking, 8, 13, 14, 15
kulans, 27

Lewa Wildlife Conservancy, *32*, 33–34

males. *See* colts; stallions.
map, *7*
Mara River, 6, 8, 9
mares, 9, 10–11, 12, 13, 15, *21*, 27
mating, 10, 13, 14
middens, 20
migration, 6, *7*, 9, *9*
Mountain Zebra National Park, 22, 34
mountain zebras, 10, 12–13, 20–22, 28, 31, 34, *35*, 37

Nairobi National Park, *30*

onagers, 27

plains zebras, 8, 10–12, *16*, 19, 20, 28
poaching, *29*, 31, 33
population, 25, 26, 27, 30, 31, 34, 37
predators, 8, 11, 15, 17, *29*, 30, 34
Przewalski's horses, *24*, 25

quaggas, 23, *23*

Serengeti Plain, 6, 8, 9, *12*
Smithsonian National Zoo, 33
species, 8, 10, 18, 20, 21, 27, 28, 32, 37
stallions, 9, 10–11, *12*, 13, 14, 15, 18
stripes, 6, 12, 15, 17, 18, 19, 20

territories, 12, 13, 20, 31
tourism, 31, 34–35

umbrella species, 31, 32
Upper Zambezi zebras, 18

weight, 15, 18, 20, 27
wild asses, 25, 26–27, *26*
wild horses, *24*, 25, *25*, 27

zoos, 17, 23, 33, 37

About the Author

Sophie Lockwood is a former teacher and a longtime writer. She writes textbooks, newspaper articles, and magazine articles. Sophie enjoys writing about animals and their habits. The most interesting part of her research, Sophie says, is learning how scientists apply their knowledge to save endangered species. She lives with her husband in the foothills of the Blue Ridge Mountains.